Who Is
Katie Ledecky?

Who Is
Katie Ledecky?

by James Buckley Jr.

illustrated by Laurie A. Conley

Penguin Workshop

For Conor and (my) Katie!—JB

PENGUIN WORKSHOP
An imprint of Penguin Random House LLC, New York

First published in the United States of America by Penguin Workshop,
an imprint of Penguin Random House LLC, New York, 2024

Visit us online at penguinrandomhouse.com.

Library of Congress Cataloging-in-Publication Data is available.

Printed in the United States of America

ISBN 9780593752845 (paperback)   10 9 8 7 6 5 4 3 2 1 WOR
ISBN 9780593752852 (library binding)   10 9 8 7 6 5 4 3 2 1 WOR

Contents

Who Is Katie Ledecky?

BONNNG! It was the women's 800-meter freestyle race at the 2012 Summer Olympics in London, and the electronic starting signal had just sent the swimmers diving into the water. Eight competitors would speed through sixteen laps in the 50-meter pool. The water splashed high into the air as the athletes swung their arms quickly.

White water churned behind them as they kicked hard over and over. When they reached each end of the pool, the swimmers did a flip, pushed off the wall, and started back.

Many of the fans who had packed into the London Aquatics Centre were born and raised in England. They were cheering for Rebecca Adlington of Great Britain, who was favored to win. She had won the gold medal in the 2008 Games and planned to defend her title. By the third lap, though, another one of the swimmers began to edge ahead of the rest. It was Katie Ledecky from the United States, and her lead grew as the athletes continued, lap after lap. With each stroke, Katie got closer to victory, even as the crowd cheered for her rival.

As she turned toward the last lap, the surprise star was far in the lead. When Katie finally touched the wall at the finish, she had set a new American record. She looked up, water dripping off her swim cap. She pulled off her goggles and looked at the scoreboard with a big smile that would soon become world-famous. She had won! At only fifteen years old, she was an Olympic champion, the second-youngest American woman ever to win an individual gold in any event! She waved at her parents, who were cheering in the stands.

"I went out fast," Katie said afterward. "I was able to hold on, and that's what I've been working on. I didn't really expect gold, but I'll take it!"

That work had started when Katie was six years old, and her continued dedication has led to one of the greatest careers in swimming history. Katie has gone from being a teen star to a seasoned veteran. Along the way, she has inspired young swimmers and teammates alike with her positive attitude and fierce determination. Let's dive in and meet one of the world's greatest swimmers!

CHAPTER 1
Future Olympian

Kathleen Ledecky was born in Washington, DC, on March 17, 1997, and grew up in Bethesda, Maryland. Her father, David, and the

rest of her family quickly nicknamed her Katie. The Ledeckys enjoyed swimming, partly because Katie's mother, Mary Gen, had been a swimmer in college. Katie's older brother, Michael, was the first to take part in swimming races. When Katie turned six, she joined Michael at the Palisades Swim & Tennis Club near the family home.

A video of six-year-old Katie shows her after her first race saying that she could not wait to race again!

Swimming was not the only sport in Katie's life. She also enjoyed watching baseball and hockey. Her uncle, Jon, was part-owner of the Washington Capitals hockey team, so she would often go to their games, hoping to see her favorite player, Adam Oates. While attending one of these games, Katie began playing peekaboo with another fan who was sitting behind her in the stands. It turned out to be National Basketball Association (NBA) legend Michael Jordan!

But Michael Jordan was not the only famous athlete Katie met when she was a child. At a swim meet when she was very young, Katie met and got an autograph from Michael Phelps, a world champion swimmer who also grew up in Maryland. For young Katie, he became an inspiration.

Michael Phelps

Like Katie Ledecky, Michael Phelps grew up in Maryland and became an international swimming star. He made his first Olympic swim in the 200-meter butterfly in 2000, but he didn't win. In 2004, he won six gold and two bronze medals, swimming freestyle, butterfly, relays, and individual medley (medley events feature a mix of swimming styles).

Four years later, at the Summer Olympics in Beijing, Michael did something no one had ever done: He won eight gold medals at one game. He also set world records in seven of those events. He added four golds and two silvers to his collection after competing in the games in 2012. For a while, Michael retired from the sport and focused on improving his mental health. But once he felt better, he decided to come back for one last time and won five more golds and a silver medal at the 2016 Summer Olympic Games.

Michael Phelps has won twenty-eight total Olympic medals, twenty-three of which are gold, making him the most decorated Olympic athlete in history.

She would get another autograph from Michael Phelps three years later. By that time Michael had become a six-time Olympic gold medalist, and he would go on to set a record for the most Olympic medals of all time.

Katie made time for other fun activities, including Irish dancing, soccer, and basketball. But she quickly found herself choosing swim practice over basketball practice if they were set at the same time. One day in fourth grade while playing basketball in gym class, Katie broke her arm. But instead of waiting until her arm was healed to swim again, she would wrap her cast in a plastic bag and kick with a kickboard in the water. Katie's passion for swimming was undeniable.

As Katie took part in more and more swim competitions, she showed the focus and dedication that would later make her a superstar. When she was only six, she began writing down swimming goals. At first, she put sticky notes on her dresser: Swim a whole lap. Reach a certain time. As her swimming improved, she wrote down more times that she wanted to aim for in different races. Katie and her brother Michael spent almost every weekend in the pool, practicing and trying to improve.

Katie joined the Nation's Capital Swim Club, where she was first coached by Yuri Suguiyama and later Bruce Gemmell. By the time Katie was in junior high, she was often beating swimmers who were in high school or college. Her coaches could see that she was something special. "Something drives them to be better every day. . . . I really don't know that it drives them to be better than their competition. I think it is something that drives them to be better than themselves," said Gemmell about athletes like Katie.

In 2011, when Katie was fourteen, she

won three events at the National Junior Championships. She was only a freshman at her high school, Stone Ridge School of the Sacred Heart, but her coaches thought she had a chance to swim in the 2012 Olympics, which would be held in London, England. Her times were good enough to earn her a spot in the 2012 US Olympic trials, an event that would be held at the end of June in Omaha, Nebraska. Athletes who performed well at that event would be selected for the US Olympic swim team.

About forty of Katie's family members came from around the country to watch her race in the trials. Most people figured that this would be the highlight of Katie's summer, just getting the chance to race among the nation's best swimmers.

In the 400-meter freestyle, Katie finished third—not high enough to win a spot on the team, though her time was America's best ever for someone aged sixteen and under. Next up was a longer race, 800 meters—sixteen laps of the 50-meter pool. It's a tough race that calls for both speed and stamina.

Katie got out in front quickly, ahead of Kate Ziegler, an older and more accomplished swimmer. To everyone's surprise, Katie won the 800-meter trial. She had made the US Olympic team! Her time of just less than 8 minutes and 20 seconds was also a new US Olympic trials record. "I knew she'd be able to do something special at Olympic trials," Coach Suguiyama said later. "I always tried to remind her: 'You belong here. This is your level.'"

While her Stone Ridge classmates went off on summer vacation, Katie Ledecky headed to London to go for the gold.

Olympic Swimming

Swimming is one of only five sports that have been part of every modern Summer Olympic Games since 1896. (The other four are cycling, fencing, gymnastics, and track and field.) Swimming events for women did not begin until 1912. Until 1908, Olympic swimming events were held in open water, including oceans, rivers, or lakes. In 2008, the Olympics brought back open-water swimming with a 10-kilometer event.

In the Summer Olympics today, swimmers compete in an indoor pool that is 50 meters long. Race distances range from 50 meters (one lap) to 1,500 meters (thirty laps). Some races are relays in which teams of four swimmers take turns. The rest are individual events.

There are four different strokes used in Summer Olympic races. In freestyle, swimmers alternate arm swings while kicking with their legs. In butterfly, the legs and arms each kick or swing together. In breaststroke, the hands come together and push backward in the water, while the legs do a frog-like kick. Backstroke is the only stroke done facing upward. While the swimmer kicks, they rotate each arm one at a time.

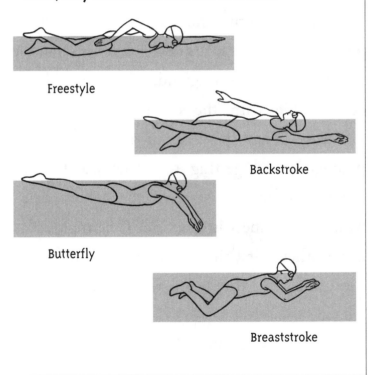

Freestyle

Backstroke

Butterfly

Breaststroke

CHAPTER 2
Suddenly a Star

Katie and her family had not expected Katie to make the Olympic team, so she and her parents had to fly to London separately. This was the first time she had traveled anywhere without her parents. While her parents scrambled to get tickets to England, Katie quickly got comfortable with the older members of the US team. They spent about a month together practicing and getting to know the Olympic coaches before the start of the games. But it wasn't all business in London. One night, Katie and other first-time Olympians performed silly skits for the team that made everyone laugh.

Katie was excited when she was given

permission to march in the opening ceremony. Most swimmers could not march because their events were just days away. Katie's first race, however, was six days after the march. So, on July 27, 2012, she paraded into London's Olympic Stadium wearing her blue jacket and beret, the official team gear, with a huge smile as she waved. Her parents, her brother, and some aunts and uncles were in the stadium, still surprised to see their Katie. She was the youngest member of the entire US Olympic team.

Once the swimming events began, Katie was able to get familiar with the Aquatics Centre. "I was lucky the 800 was later in the meet, because I was able to scope things out, watch the other swimmers race, and cheer them on," she said later. "That was the most fun part—cheering on some of the people I used to cheer on from behind the TV screen."

Katie qualified to swim in the final of the 800-meter freestyle race after doing well in preliminary rounds. When the starting tone for the final race went off, Katie dove into the water confidently. In the 800, most swimmers don't start out very fast; they know they need energy for the long race. Katie surprised everyone by sprinting the first few laps. She was in front after only three laps. Halfway through the race, at 400 meters, she had swum faster than she ever had.

But could she keep her pace up?

Later, Katie joked that she used a little imagination for motivation. The English fans were cheering "Beck-y, Beck-y" for their hero Rebecca Adlington, who had won this event at the last Summer Olympics. So Katie said she pretended they were saying "Le-DECK-y, Le-DECK-y!"

Katie pulled farther and farther ahead, telling herself, "Hold on, Katie! Hold on! Don't let anyone pass you." As she pushed off from the wall after a lap late in the race, she saw other swimmers were just getting to the wall. That's when she knew all she needed to do was finish strong.

And she did. She was an Olympic champion!

A neighbor from Maryland tossed an American flag to Katie as the medal ceremony began. Her parents and brother watched from nearby seats as Katie stood for the national anthem, the gold medal around her neck and the American flag in her hands.

Afterward, Katie was grateful. She knew how much help she had received to reach her goals. "I couldn't have done any of this without everyone's support—my family, teammates, coaches, everyone at [Church of the] Little Flower, Stone Ridge, and my neighborhood—all cheering me on and watching. It means so much to me," she said.

Not long after the London Games were over, Katie went back to school and to her swim club where she had even more people supporting her. Over three hundred classmates and teachers at Stone Ridge School watched Katie's events at a special assembly. She even answered some questions her classmates had. They were thrilled that one of their friends had a chance to be a champion. It was the start of an amazing period for Katie. A year after the Olympics, at the 2013 World Aquatics Championships, she set her first world records—in the 800- and 1,500-meter freestyle races. At the same meet, she helped the American team win the 4 x 200-meter relay. She was also named the US Olympic Committee Sportswoman of the Year.

Even as she balanced her schoolwork and friendships with workouts and travel, Katie was breaking more barriers. By the end of 2014, she had become the first woman since American star Janet Evans to hold, at the same time, world records for the 400-, 800-, and 1,500-meter freestyle races.

One event shows just how talented Katie was. In the 1,500-meter race at the 2014 Pan Pacific Championships, she beat her own previous world record by six seconds. Most new records are set by less than a second each time. She finished *twenty-seven seconds* ahead of the second-place swimmer; she was more than a lap ahead of three other swimmers. No one could keep up with Katie in the pool.

When she wasn't winning races, Katie tried to have a regular high school life. She still swam for her school team and took part in their "Gator Chomp" cheer after races. She and her mom began to collect and preserve her swimming memories, putting letters from heroes into plastic sleeves, and arranging medals and trophies on shelves. Her brother stopped trying to swim against her, though!

Also, in 2014, she and her family shared a special moment at another pool. A ceremony was held to name a new Olympic-size pool in Williston, North Dakota, after Katie's grandfather, Bud Hagan. Katie had the honor of swimming the first lap while her family cheered her on. Katie said it meant as much as winning Olympic gold.

Katie's success continued at the 2015 World Aquatics Championships. She won five gold medals (one on a relay squad), and became the only swimmer ever to win four individual freestyle events at a single championship. One of them came in the 200-meter freestyle—at only four laps, a shorter event usually won by sprinters. Katie was showing that she could win at almost any distance, a rare achievement for a swimmer. Later, in the 1,500-meter race, she was so far ahead that she finished before all the other swimmers had even started their last lap!

That same year, Katie achieved another milestone; she graduated from high school!

As great as she was doing in her swimming career, Katie knew she could do better. Heading toward the 2016 Olympics in Rio de Janeiro, Brazil, Katie continued to set goals as she had done when she was younger. On a buoy that floated in her practice pool, she wrote the numbers 565. The numbers were part of the times she wanted to reach in the 400- and 800-meter races, respectively: 3:56 and 8:05. By having them always in front of her, she could focus on what she needed to do to get better. "Obviously, you can't just throw out crazy numbers and have that become a reality," she said later. "But I think there's something to be said for the fact that I looked at those numbers every day."

As she had always done, Katie rose to the moment. She won four gold medals and a silver medal in Rio. As for those times she was aiming for? She matched or beat both of her goal times! In some 800 races, the difference between first and second place can be less than a second. Katie won in Rio by an incredible *11.38* seconds!

She won the 200-meter freestyle race for the first time at an Olympics, and also earned a silver medal with her American teammates in the 4 x 100-meter relay.

In another race, the 4 x 200-meter freestyle relay, the US team trailed Australia by just over a second as Katie dove in for the final laps. She caught up to the leader and brought home the gold for Team USA! As she had in earlier Olympics, Katie was inspired by her fellow Maryland swim star, Michael Phelps. He did pretty well himself in 2016, winning five golds, the most by any athlete that year.

"[Phelps has] had a huge impact on . . . a lot

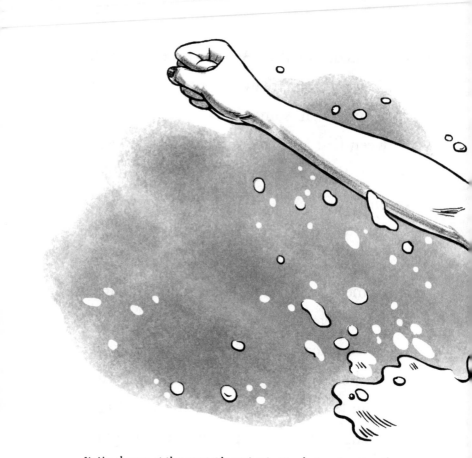
Katie cheers at the 2016 Olympics in Rio de Janeiro, Brazil

of the young swimmers on the team this year," Ledecky said. "To be on the team with him has been such an honor." Katie and Michael even re-created the photo of Michael signing an autograph for Katie that was taken ten years

earlier. But this time, instead of Michael sitting at the autograph table, Katie sat and signed a Rio poster for Michael.

Katie enjoyed her Rio Olympics experience in and out of the pool. "I had a ton of fun," she said. "I had my goals in the water, but one of those goals was also just to have fun, and I couldn't have asked for a better time here with my teammates."

CHAPTER 3
Stanford Success

In the fall of 2016, Katie entered Stanford University in California. She had been accepted after graduating high school a year earlier, but she put off attending to take part in the 2016 Olympics. After Rio, she had a chance to become a professional swimmer, but she wanted the college experience.

With Michael's retirement, Katie was the biggest swimming star in the world, but she acted just like any other student at Stanford. She shared a room in the freshman dorm with three other roommates, and she practiced swimming with her college teammates Her coach, Greg Meehan, remembered that Katie did all the drills and workouts "just the same as the freshman who walked in the door without having ever made an international team."

Katie was not only focused on swimming at Stanford. She took classes in art history and psychology, even telling the story of the buoy

with the numbers on it in a class that was studying motivation.

Katie also found time to have fun, visiting children in a nearby hospital to bring the patients some cheer and playing the saxophone in the school's marching band.

Katie got to brush up on her bicycling skills, too. She didn't have much time to ride as a kid, but a bike was the best way to get around Stanford's large green campus, where she lived.

Being famous did have some rewards; Katie was able to meet important visitors to Stanford, and once even gave a swimming lesson to Facebook founder Mark Zuckerberg.

Katie was still able to swim independently as well as for Stanford's team. At the 2017 World Aquatics Championships, Katie won five more gold medals and a silver, giving her more career world championship medals than any female swimmer in history.

In the spring of 2018, Katie helped Stanford win another national championship, winning two races and helping on a winning relay. She ended her college swimming career with four National Collegiate Athletics Association (NCAA) Division I records and eight national individual championship wins.

Not long after her final meet at Stanford, Katie became a professional swimmer. That meant she could earn money for racing, even while still studying at Stanford. Throughout 2018, she took part in professional swimming races around the country. Katie took her books and schoolwork with her and went to classes online or in between meets. She was also able to sign up with sponsors who paid her to wear their swim gear or clothing. That year, twenty-one-year-old Katie signed her first sponsorship deal, with a swimwear company called TYR Sport. Some reports say she earned $7 million in that deal.

By 2019, Katie was nearly ready to graduate from Stanford, but she decided to take a break from her studies to prepare for the next Olympics, scheduled for Tokyo, Japan, in the summer of 2020.

CHAPTER 4
Triumph in Tokyo

In March 2020, however, the disease known as COVID-19 spread across the world, causing a pandemic with millions of deaths. To try to prevent the disease from spreading even more, many countries instructed their citizens to stay indoors. They also closed their borders so people could not travel. Because of this, sporting events, including the Tokyo Olympics, had to be canceled or postponed. Like everyone else, Katie had to adjust her plans. Showing the same drive she put into her swimming, she found a way to make the terrible circumstances work for her. Instead of taking the year off school, she signed back up for online classes at Stanford. (One of her classes studied the effect of the pandemic on world events!) She also decided to live in the Bay Area to be near school and her college classmates.

Katie stayed in swimming shape by using a friend's backyard pool. She was joined by fellow Olympian Simone Manuel—and the friend's three young grandchildren. Katie joked that she sometimes got distracted by one of the kids riding a pink bicycle. She also continued a tradition that had started when she was little—Katie always has a glass of chocolate milk not long after each workout is over. When she was not swimming, she kept earning credits from Stanford toward a degree in psychology with a minor in political science.

Still, the time during the pandemic was hard. Katie was lonely and missed her family, whom she hadn't seen for over a year. One way she connected with her family was through virtual phone calls. On Sundays, they would join a video call and live stream church services. Katie's Catholic faith was very important to her, and it called her to help others in need.

During the 2016 Olympics, Katie had learned about the Refugee Olympic Team. Refugees are people who are unable to return to their home countries because of war, violence, or other dangers. Katie was inspired by their stories, especially because her grandfather had been a refugee from the former Czechoslovakia after World War II. In 2021, she began working with the Jesuit Refugee Service to raise awareness about the global refugee crisis. "I think everyone deserves to have a place to call home," she said later.

By the summer of 2021, Katie moved from fun practices in a backyard pool to tougher workouts in the Stanford University pool so she would be ready for the games in Tokyo. She easily qualified for the 2021 US team at the Olympic trials in June. Katie was not able to attend her college graduation ceremony in person because it took place while she was in Nebraska for the trials, but she joined through a video call from her hotel room.

Katie earned places on the US team in all four distance freestyle events: 200-, 400-, 800-, and 1,500-meter races. After she finished the 400-meter race, she and her family shared a hug for the first time in more than a year. "After the finals of the 400 we were able to get a group hug. It was very emotional and a relief we had gotten to that point. It was very special," said Mary Gen Ledecky.

Katie had to go to Tokyo without her family to cheer her on. Because of the pandemic, fans were not allowed into Japan. Katie also faced a tough schedule: She was set to swim ten races in only seven days. It would be a lot of work, but she was used to it. Katie also faced tougher competition in Tokyo than ever before, but she came through with two more gold medals and two silvers. The 1,500-meter race for women was held for the first time as an Olympic event, and Katie won gold.

The Refugee Olympic Team

How can an athlete compete in the Olympic Games if they have no country to support them? That is the problem faced by refugee athletes, and they often have a hard time continuing their careers.

In 2016, the Olympics created the first Refugee Team. The International Olympic Committee provided more than forty refugee athletes with support and places to train. Athletes came from places such as Ethiopia, South Sudan, and Syria. The ten best performers earned spots on the team and competed at the games in Brazil. They participated in swimming, judo, and track and field.

There were also Refugee Teams in the 2020 and 2024 Summer Games.

The Refugee Olympic Team at the Summer Olympics
in Tokyo, Japan, 2021

"She's already the greatest female swimmer in history, bar none," said former Olympian and swimming analyst Rowdy Gaines. "It's not even close anymore."

Katie wrapped up her 2021 Olympics with another gold medal in the 800-meter race. It was her seventh gold overall. She was so dominant in the 800 meters that all thirty of the fastest times ever swum in that event were set by Katie.

When reporters asked how she felt about the games, Katie said, "It's an amazing feeling to be . . . competing in my third Olympics. Even though we had to be super careful and wear masks and do [COVID-19] tests, it still felt really good to be all together and race against the fastest swimmers in the world."

After returning from Japan, she spent time with her family in Maryland, and she also made time to visit her old school in Maryland and tell students about her adventures and career.

In late 2021, Katie left California and moved to Florida to serve as a volunteer assistant coach for the University of Florida Gators. She also trained with the team's head coach, Anthony Nesty. Her training paid off, because she won four more gold medals at the 2022 World Aquatics Championships.

In 2023, Katie broke yet another world record. She became the only swimmer to win six world championship gold medals in the same event when she won the 800-meter final race again. This win also helped her set an all-time record of sixteen individual world championship gold medals, breaking a tie with Phelps.

Of course, Katie has more goals written down. This includes doing well at the 2024 Olympic Games in Paris, France. Is there more gold

in Katie's future? Whatever happens, Katie Ledecky is a phenomenal athlete who has already won the hearts of millions of fans across the world.

Timeline of Katie Ledecky's Life

1997 — Kathleen Ledecky is born March 17 in Bethesda, Maryland

2003 — Begins swimming at a local pool

2011 — Wins National Junior Championships in 400-, 800-, and 1,500-meter races

2012 — Wins first Olympic gold medal in 800 meters in the London Games

2013 — Sets first world records, in 800- and 1,500-meter races

2015 — Sets record with four individual freestyle gold-medal wins at the World Aquatics Championships

2016 — Wins four gold medals and a silver at the Rio Olympics

— Attends Stanford University to study psychology

2017 — Helps win first of two NCAA swimming championships

2021 — Wins two golds and two silvers at Tokyo Olympics

2023 — Wins record-breaking sixteenth individual gold medal at the World Aquatics Championships

Timeline of the World

1997	The first Harry Potter book is published in England
2001	Terrorists crash planes into buildings in New York City and Washington, DC
2005	Hurricane Katrina causes damage on the Gulf Coast of the United States
2007	The iPhone is introduced to the world by Apple
2008	Barack Obama is elected as the first Black president of the United States
2010	The Burj Khalifa opens in Dubai, becoming the tallest building in the world at 163 stories
2011	Starting in Tunisia, the movement known as Arab Spring spreads across the Middle East, as citizens call for change and the elimination of government corruption
2016	Almost two hundred countries sign the Paris Agreement, promising to take steps soon to ease climate change
2020	The COVID-19 pandemic spreads around the world, killing millions of people and creating economic problems
2022	Russia invades the neighboring country of Ukraine

Bibliography

*Books for young readers

*Fishman, Jon M. *Katie Ledecky (Sports All-Stars)*. Minneapolis:
Lerner Sports: 2021.

"Katie Ledecky." *Sports Illustrated Kids*. Accessed December 1,
2023. www.sikids.com/tag/katie-ledecky.

"Katie Ledecky." *SwimSwam*. Accessed December 1, 2023. www.
swimswam.com/bio/katie-ledecky/.

*Mattern, Joanne. *Sports Report: 12 Reasons to Love Swimming*.
Mankato, MN: 12-Story Library, 2021.

*Price, Karen. *GOATs of Olympics Sports*. Minneapolis:
SportsZone, 2021.